little backyard animals

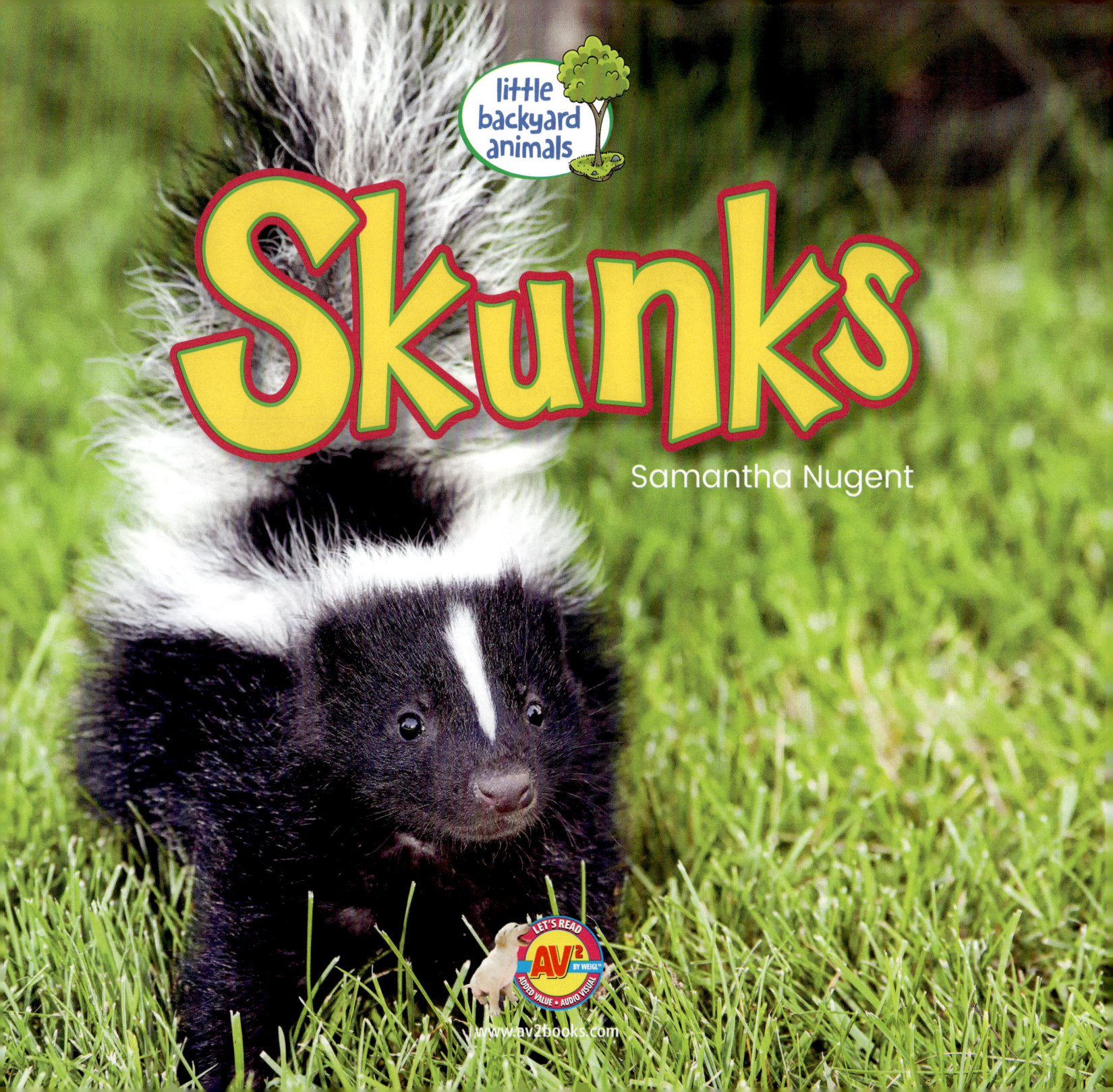

Skunks

Samantha Nugent

www.av2books.com

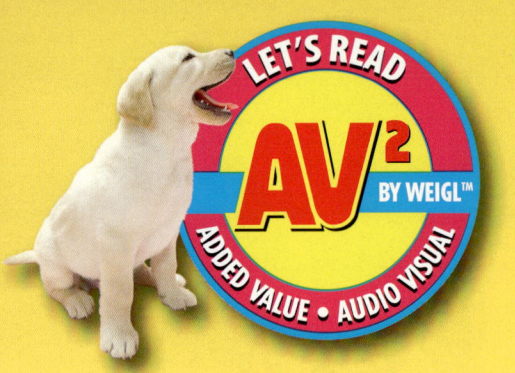

AV² provides enriched content that supplements and complements this book. Weigl's AV² books strive to create inspired learning and engage young minds in a total learning experience.

Your AV² Media Enhanced books come alive with...

Audio
Listen to sections of the book read aloud.

Video
Watch informative video clips.

Embedded Weblinks
Gain additional information for research.

Try This!
Complete activities and hands-on experiments.

Key Words
Study vocabulary, and complete a matching word activity.

Quizzes
Test your knowledge.

Slide Show
View images and captions, and prepare a presentation.

... and much, much more!

Go to www.av2books.com, and enter this book's unique code.

BOOK CODE

G796333

AV² by Weigl brings you media enhanced books that support active learning.

Published by AV² by Weigl
350 5th Avenue, 59th Floor New York, NY 10118
Website: www.av2books.com

Copyright ©2017 AV² by Weigl
All rights reserved. No part of this publication may be reproduced, stored in a retrieval system, or transmitted in any form or by any means, electronic, mechanical, photocopying, recording, or otherwise, without the prior written permission of Weigl Publishers Inc.

Library of Congress Control Number: 2015958798

ISBN 978-1-4896-4755-9 (hardcover)
ISBN 978-1-4896-4813-6 (softcover)
ISBN 978-1-4896-4756-6 (multi-user eBook)

Printed in the United States of America in Brainerd, Minnesota
1 2 3 4 5 6 7 8 9 0 19 18 17 16 15

122015
041215

Project Coordinator: Heather Kissock
Designer: Terry Paulhus

Every reasonable effort has been made to trace ownership and to obtain permission to reprint copyright material. The publisher would be pleased to have any errors or omissions brought to its attention so that they may be corrected in subsequent printings.

The publisher acknowledges Corbis Images, Getty Images, Shutterstock, Minden Pictures, Alamy, and iStock as the primary image suppliers for this title.

Skunks

In this book, I will tell you about their

home   **food**

family

and **how they grow up.**

One spring day, I was playing in the backyard with my sister. We saw something walking along our deck. It looked like a black and white cat.

When the cat went under the deck, we called our mom to come outside. She took a look and started laughing. She told us it was a skunk, not a cat.

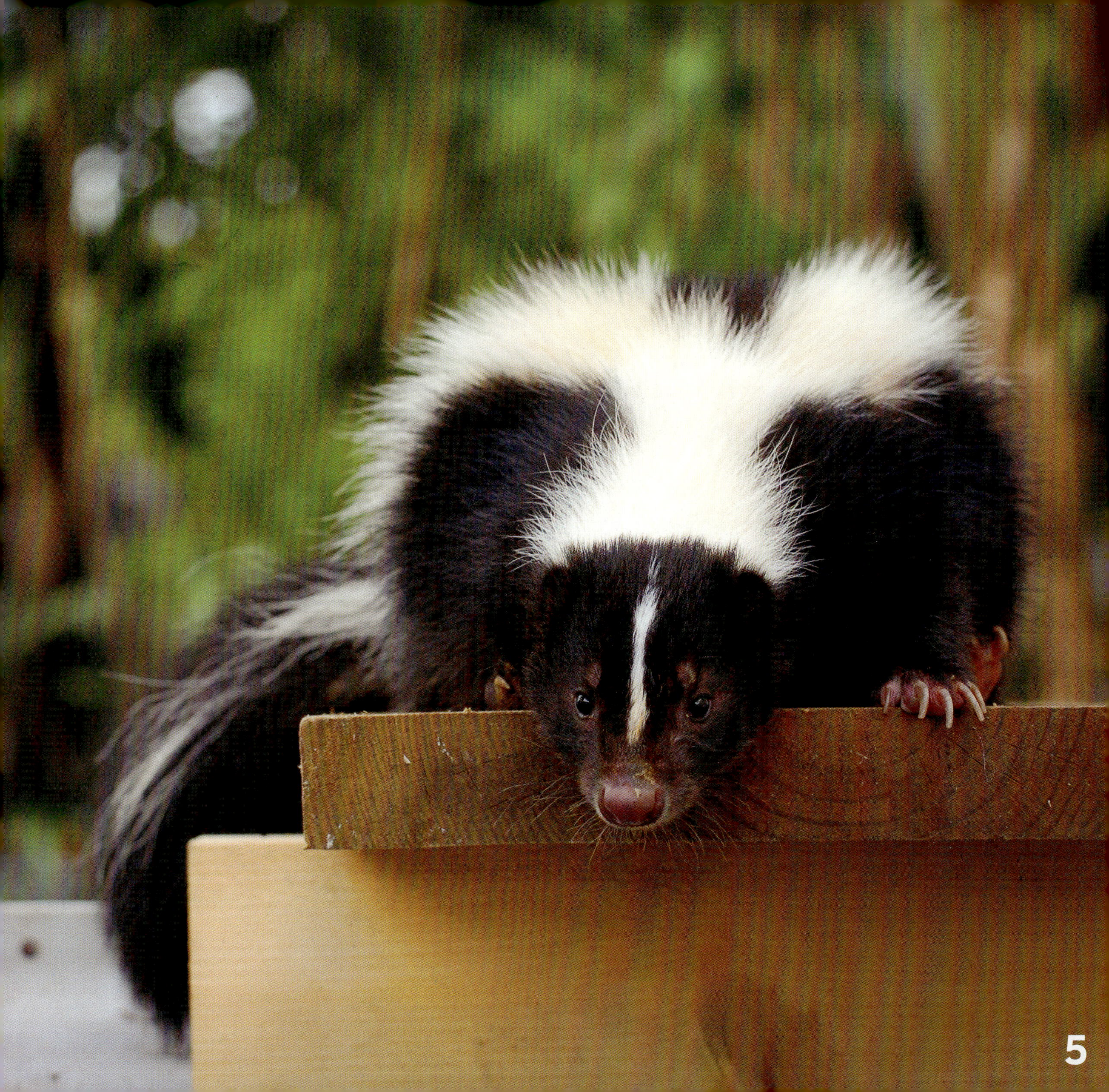

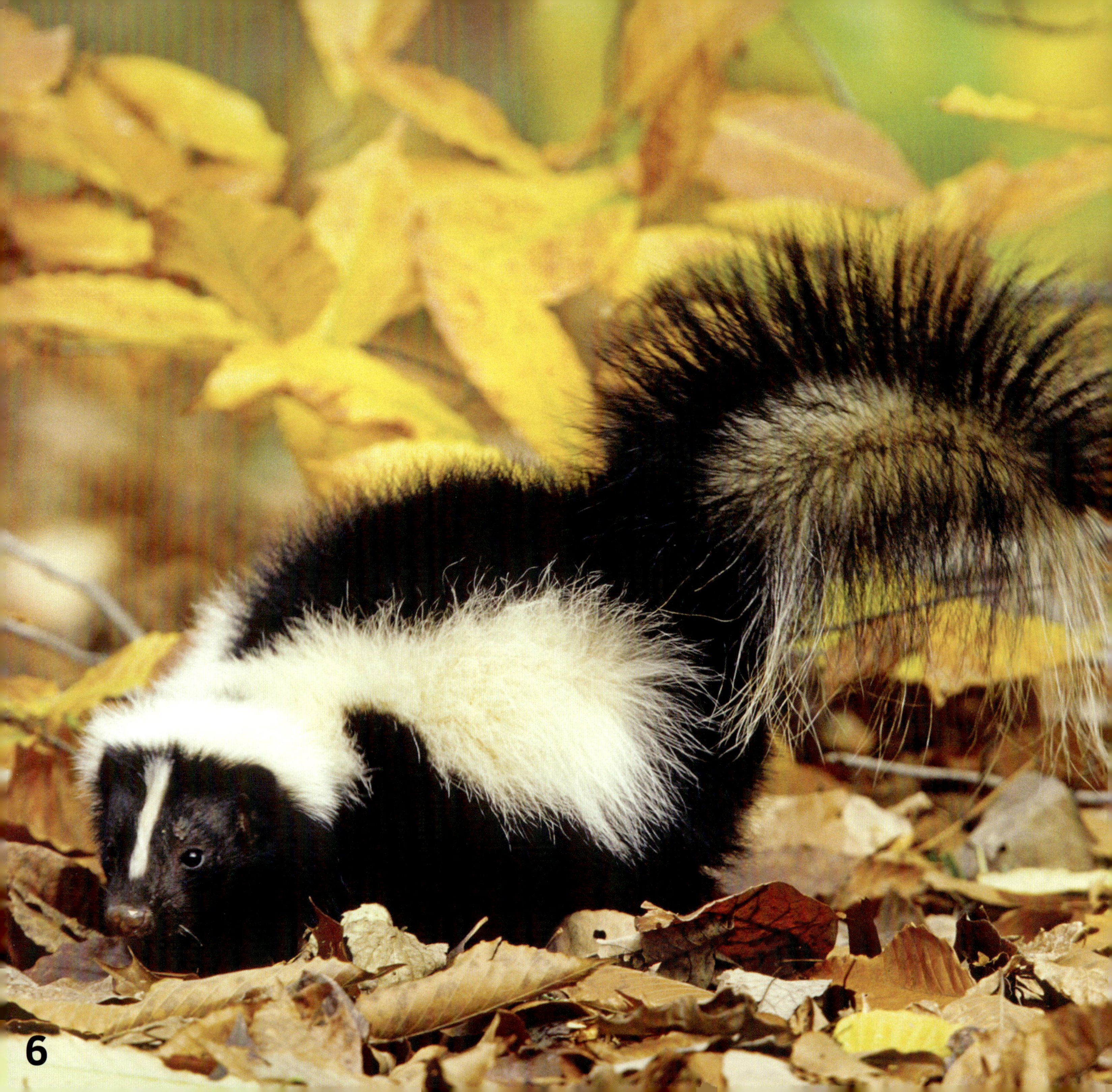

The skunk had pulled a bunch of leaves and grass under the deck. It had put them in a big pile. Mom said the skunk was making a nest.

Mom told us that skunks spray a bad smell when they feel afraid. She said we should give the skunk lots of space so that it would feel safe.

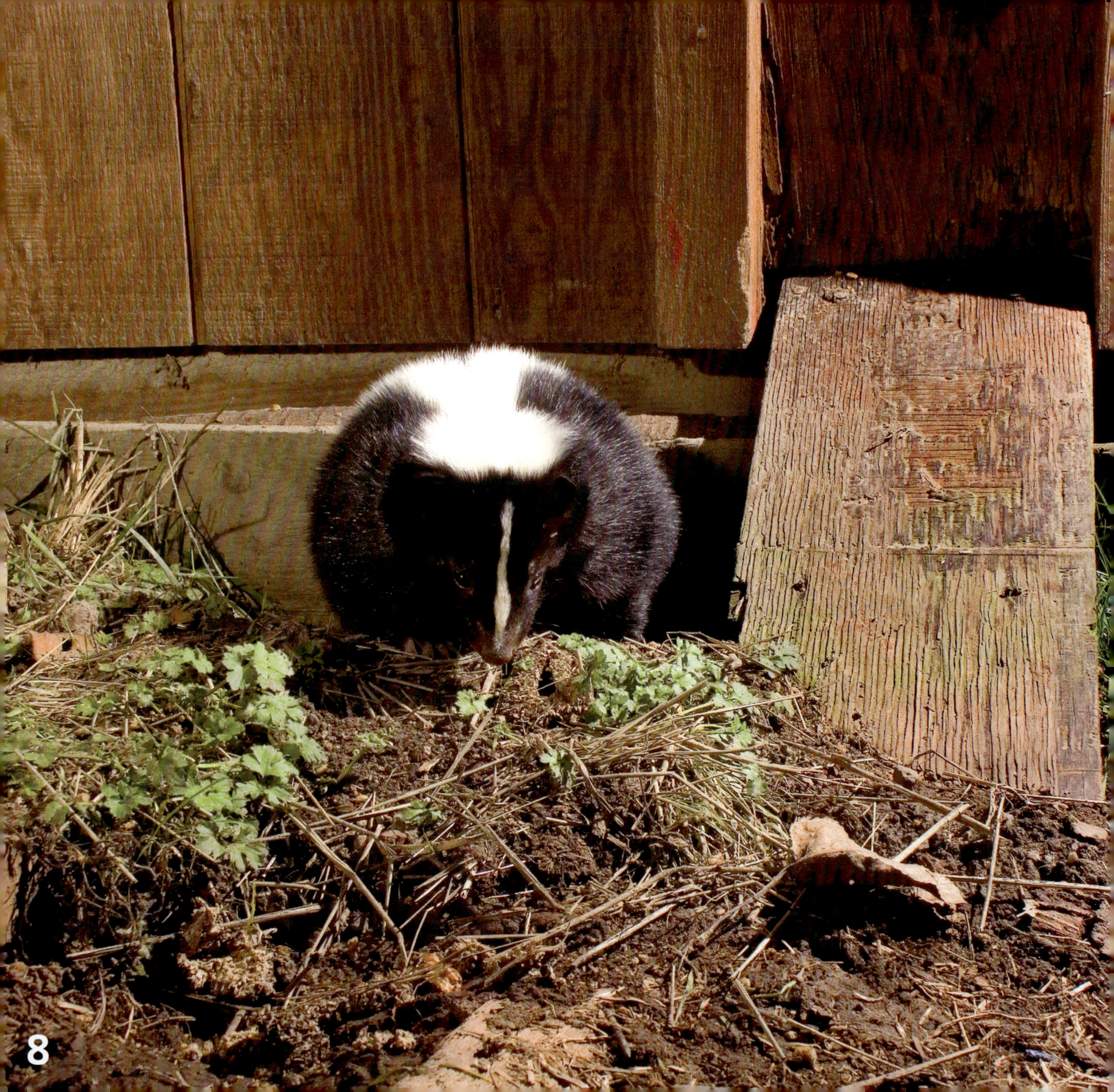

One night, our mom called us to the window. We could see the skunk digging near the shed. It ate some bugs and went back under the deck.

Our mom said skunks do not often stay in one nest for that long. She thought the skunk might have had babies.

My sister and I looked for the skunk every day. We wanted to see her babies.

Sometimes, we saw the skunk during the day. She mostly came out at night.

11

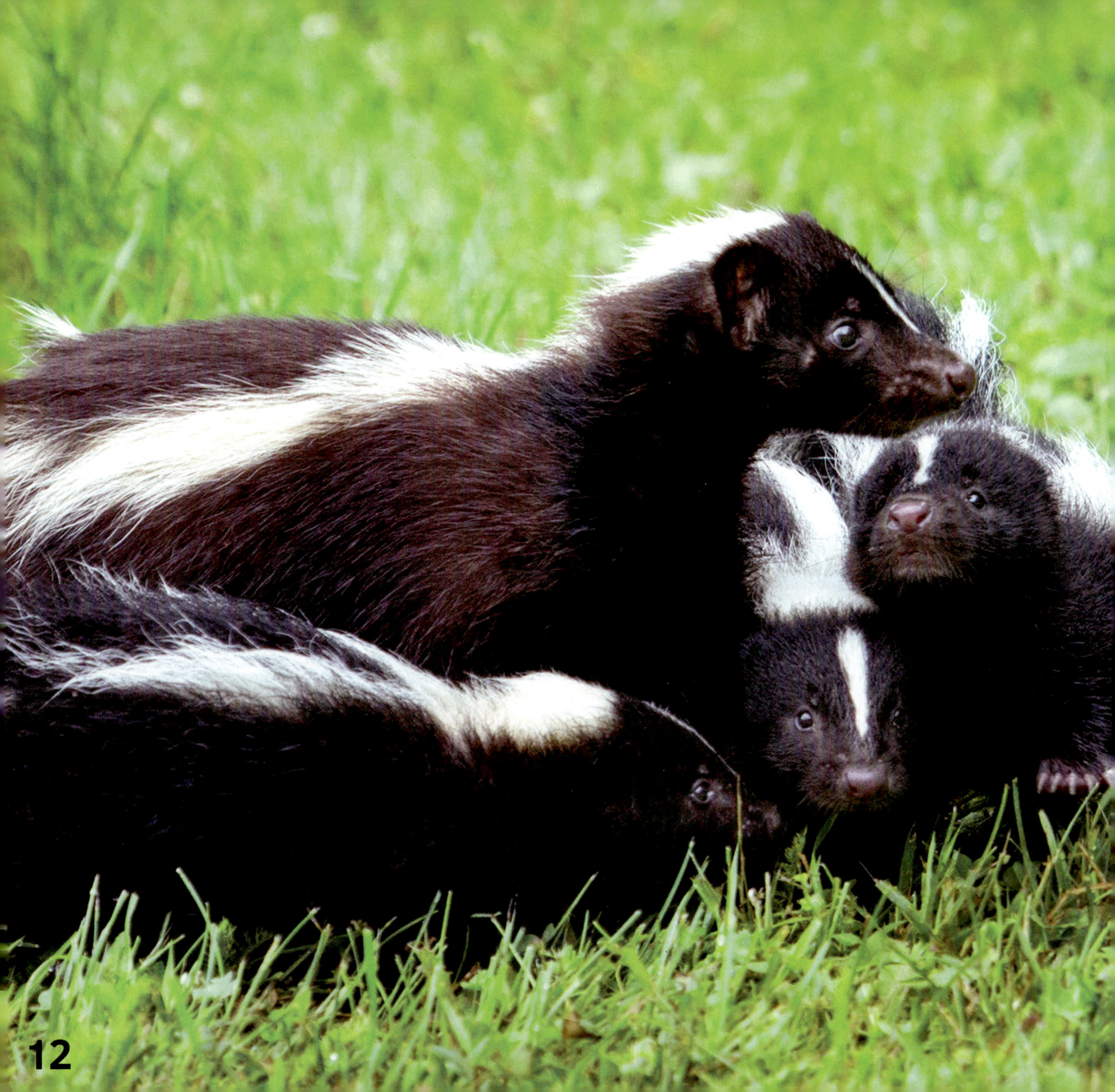

After two whole months, we finally saw six little babies. They looked like black and white kittens.

The babies wrestled and played together in the grass.

14

Any time we saw the mother skunk, we also saw her babies. They went everywhere together.

The mother would walk in front, and her babies would follow in a line behind her.

The skunk was a very good mother. She showed her babies where to find food in the yard.

I saw her show the babies where to find bugs and plants to eat.

17

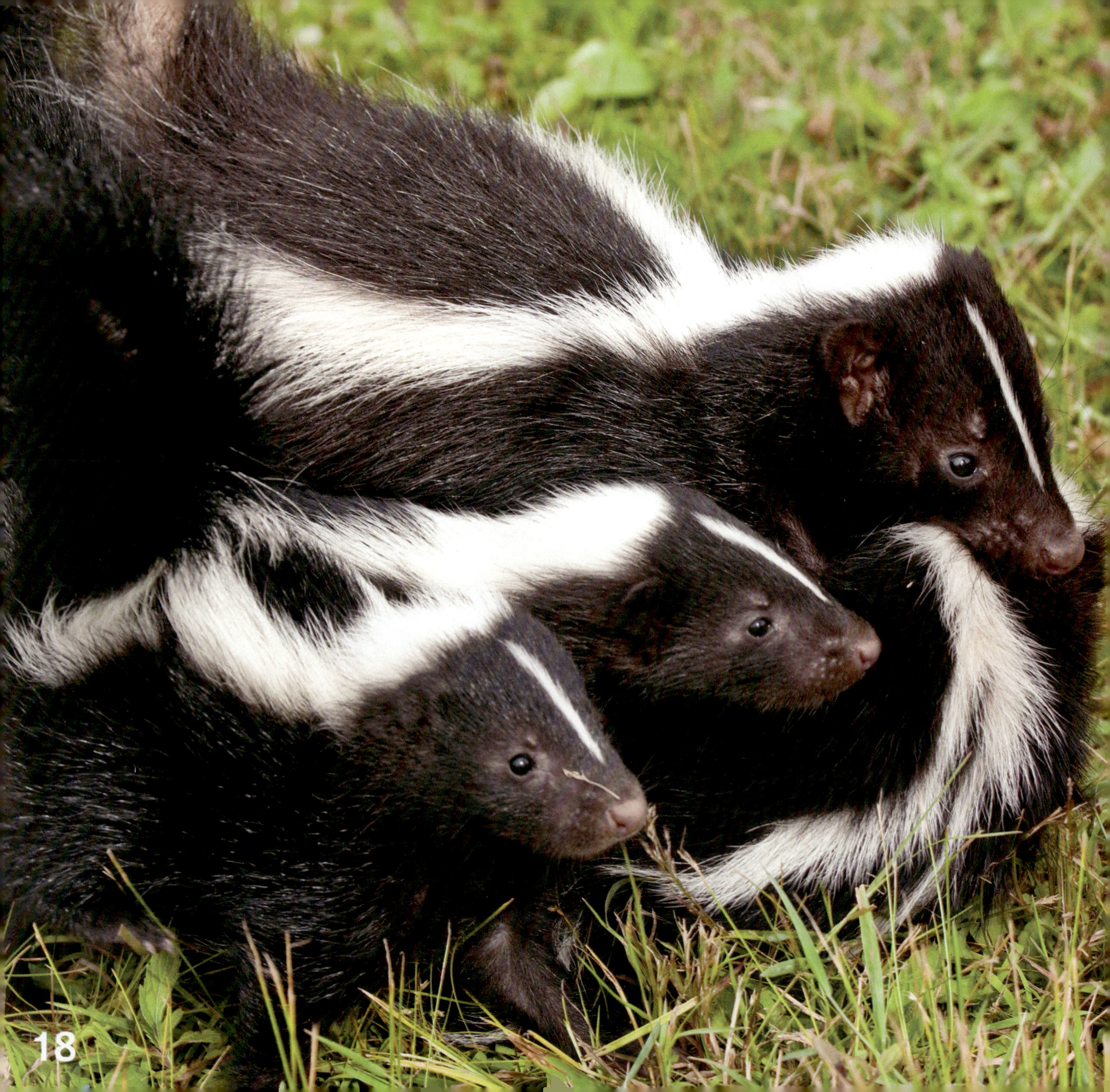

The babies grew up quickly.
By the end of the summer,
they were almost as big as
their mother.

They could find food
all on their own.

Just before school was about to start, the skunks disappeared. We could not find them anywhere.

Our mom said the babies had grown big enough to find their own homes.

21

The next spring, we saw little paw prints in the garden.

We looked under the deck.
Another skunk had come
to live in our backyard.

KEY WORDS

Research has shown that as much as 65 percent of all written material published in English is made up of 300 words. These 300 words cannot be taught using pictures or learned by sounding them out. They must be recognized by sight. This book contains 97 common sight words to help young readers improve their reading fluency and comprehension. This book also teaches young readers several important content words, such as proper nouns. These words are paired with pictures to aid in learning and improve understanding.

Page	Sight Words First Appearance
4	a, along, and, come, day, I, in, it, like, look, my, not, one, our, saw, she, something, started, take, the, to, took, under, us, was, we, went, when, white, with
7	big, give, had, leaves, of, put, said, should, so, that, them, they, would
9	back, could, do, for, have, long, might, near, night, often, see, some, thought
10	at, came, every, her, sometimes
13	after, little, together, two
15	also, any, line, mother, time
16	eat, find, food, good, plants, show, very, where
19	all, almost, as, by, end, on, own, their, up, were
20	about, before, enough, homes, just, school
22	next
23	another, live

Page	Content Words First Appearance
4	backyard, cat, deck, mom, sister, skunk
7	bunch, grass, nest, pile, smell, space
9	babies, bugs, shed, window
13	kittens, months
16	yard
19	summer
22	garden, paw prints, spring

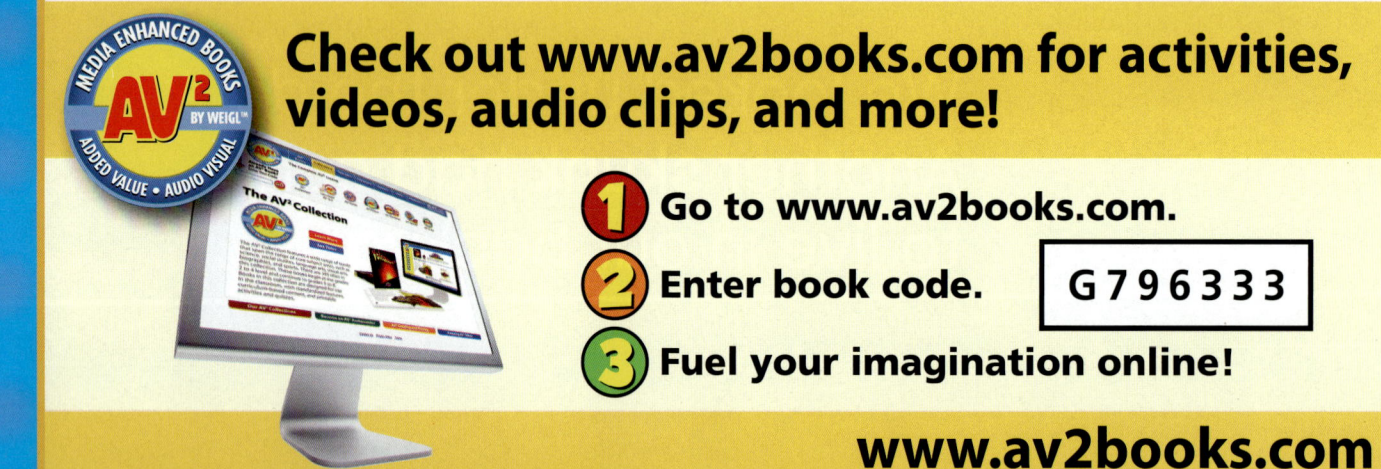

Check out www.av2books.com for activities, videos, audio clips, and more!

1. Go to www.av2books.com.
2. Enter book code. G796333
3. Fuel your imagination online!

www.av2books.com